TAKING
TO WATER

Also by Roberta Spear

SILKS

TAKING
TO WATER

Poems by
ROBERTA SPEAR

An Owl Book
HOLT, RINEHART AND WINSTON
NEW YORK

First published in January 1985 by Holt, Rinehart and Winston,
383 Madison Avenue, New York, New York 10017.

Published simultaneously in Canada by Holt, Rinehart and
Winston of Canada, Limited.

Library of Congress Cataloging in Publication Data
Spear, Roberta.
Taking to water.
"An Owl Book."
I. Title.
PS3569.P395T3   1984   811'.54   84-4676
ISBN 0-03-000509-4

First Edition

Design by Dalia Bergsagel
Printed in the United States of America
1   3   5   7   9   10   8   6   4   2

These poems originally appeared in the following publications:

The American Poetry Review: "Chartres" and "Men Back Then"; *The
Antioch Review*: "The Prisoners of Loches"; *The Iowa Review*: "Fishes at
Saint-Jean*: Chagall, 1949"; *The Memphis Review*: "Two Trees," "The Old
City," "Map for the Unborn," and "The Moravian Cemetery: 'God's
Acre'"; *The New Yorker*: "Catfish" and "Diving for Atlantis"; *Poetry*: "Oi-
dle-doi-dle-doi," "Ice," and "Cinque Terre: The Land of Five Noises";
Raccoon: "Cotton"; *Sage*: "Rue Madame"; *The Southern Poetry Review*: "The
Last Gift."

"*Fishes at Saint-Jean*: Chagall, 1949" also appeared in the anthology *Extended
Outlooks*, Collier Books, 1982.

I would like to thank the National Endowment for the Arts for a grant that
enabled me to complete this book. I would also like to thank Robert Hedin
and Peter Everwine for their help.

ISBN 0-03-000509-4

For Jeff and Eli

CONTENTS

• *This symbol is used to indicate a space between stanzas*
of a poem wherever such spaces are lost in pagination.

PART ONE

DIVING FOR ATLANTIS

for Ada

In a flush of leafless gum and alder,
the old Fourth Street Y
where the run-off from swamps
and secret southern tides collects.
On cold afternoons,
the black kids come here to dive
for what one says is *Atlanta,*
an island floating miles beneath
the fractured basin of this pool,
loaded with all the precious stones
their mothers promised them
in lullabies. Like the gulls
or kingfishers cracking the slate swells
200 miles from here, down they go
shooting up again and again
through the wreath of bubbles
to the surface, screaming
found it, found it.

Who in this city
smelling of scorched tobacco
and hickory dust would believe
what they can't see or sell,
so much water slipping through fingers?
Like the old woman lounging
on a faded towel, winter settles
into an armchair padded with dead leaves
and counts its treasure—
all the white faces glistening like dimes,
all the blacks bearing out
the same cold. But here,
a child in a pair of scissored trousers

leaps into the water and learns
to hold his breath until
the vision comes and the sunlight
slices him into every color.

Lady, the woman tells me, *Methodists
don't take to water,
but I'm learning.
It's the Baptists who walk into lakes
and leave the rest of us
standing on the shore.*

And I believe that even hers,
the heaviest earthbound body,
can hold air and float
on those seven veils of blue.
When I plunge headfirst,
joining her and all the others,
my flesh steeps and the steam rises
off the surface. I believe
that those who swim in winter
shed ghosts like these
whose sweet alum tears fall
to something larger, a sea
that never freezes over,
whose gentle pulse carries them
away from the Y, from this city,
to the shores of Atlanta
where, when they surface,
they will send for us.

ICE

There were no leaves,
no insects curled inside the flower pots,
no ravens on the feeder.
No mufflers snorted *death-be-gone,*
for the road had slipped away.
For the old had stiffened in their chairs
by fires that were blue and hidden.
The wires were stunned,
the children's swings unhooked,
the sky between them gone.
Only a shawl of fog dragged the icy field.

A day as white as the milk
the blind pour. A silence stretched
from the fingertips into the world.
But slowly, my fingers let go.
I focused on a tassel,
clumps of wild onion here and there,
stronger than ice.
And, out of nowhere, a circle of footprints
nearly reached our door.

I imagined the rubbed seams
of your pockets, your shoulders
slumped from the weight of that shawl,
each frightened breath
saved for someone more powerful.
When night came, we rolled full-weight
together and listened to the thaw,
the loose chunks slipping

from the northern shingles. And further up,
to the last beast tiptoeing
over that dark plain where ice belongs.

CATFISH

By 6 A.M., the catfish
freshened on ice
have lost their pallor
and look like something
you'd want to eat.
A line snakes through the shadows
down Trade Street
where the last person stoops
to read the paper he brought
to wrap his fish in.
It takes pliers to open
a catfish plugged with tin and algae.
But the small ones, delicate,
dipped in batter,
are like white roses
blooming on grease.

I don't know what the sun
will mean to this winter day,
already sinking into the brick
and steam. But those who've left
their beds, their children,
their frozen corners
to stand in line outside the market,
hope it will shine forever,
radiant as the gaze of one
who swims through both mud and ink.

My friend feeds more sticks
to the fire and the flames jump

to the stained kettle of greens.
She tells me a dream she had
of a vacant strand on the Outer Banks,
and a flounder she found
with both faces up to the sun.
When she flicked it over
with another stick,
she saw her eyes, her own
slow smile, even her soul scattered
by gulls on the ribbons of sand.

Now she can't eat fish—
even catfish
which will eat anything.

In the dawn, mine is the only face
that loses its darkness.
I place my change on the glass
and reach into the strange aquarium
where the fish are stacked
in even numbers. Their fins
and whiskers are touching
as though they still know
who loves and hates them.

In the South,
fish are cooked in lard,
lard in greens, and greens
in warm silty water.
And when rings rise
to the unbroken surface,

then you know it is true.
The stars move to another pond,
and a mewing starts up
in the trees.

TOBACCO

The sun behind us, we follow
a flatbed into town.
On a bed of tobacco, two men are asleep
and when the bales lurch
they wedge their fingers under the wire,
getting a firmer grip
on the warm golden leaves.

Tonight, the last stalks bow
to the river and its broken songs.
But in the lighted factories,
the harvest rises again,
fire and steam pressing the heavy scent
into the air. So strong
it comes between us as we sleep.

The auctioneer known for his large voice
spits out the dust and begins
the long painful story:
men and women, new crops sold for paper
worth nothing in the end.

Instead, I would like to witness
the dispersal of sunlight
on the raked fields, the sweet blades
defending themselves, the lives
like sugar rushing up through shallow roots
to take back what is theirs.

We learn young to distrust
certain kinds of seduction—men dozing
in daylight, women who poison
their gentle parts.

My grandmother told me
she put tobacco to her own lips
only once in her life,
to please a man
who tipped the brown flakes
into the thin fold of paper.
He promised no other worlds—
only many stories with
many endings.

COTTON

The moon rolls down on the sour marshes
of the coast. Out there,
a child going home on foot
sees the first spiked flowers rise
out of their icy pods
toward the light, each one
holding the dream of cotton.

Like a sharecropper's child, you sleep
in all your clothes or none.
Each night, I shake the flannel sheet
and wrap you in it—
a moth flutters up, in love
with your pale skin.
When I was young, I loved
a skirt woven in coarse emerald cotton
by women whose fingers flew over the loom,
dropping bits of green yarn
into their children's mouths. The vein
of silver zigzagging through the hem
brought luck to the oldest.
They told me I could wear that skirt
to heaven and gather flowers
all winter with the saints.

But only the weaver's palms
etched with stars of blood
can choose their dreams.
In the shop of pieced goods,
the bolts stacked beyond reach

like the remnants of those saints.
Before their dyes and velvet naps,
we remember little.
Even less after the collar frays
and the pocket swallows the light
of everything it holds.
I give them all away, in a box
someone will find on the curb one night
when the moon is wound tight again
and a thin silver steeple
whipstitches the skies together.

TWO TREES

This summer they are saying
that two trees which never did before
swayed toward each other,
mingling leaves.
Shedding their powders at the same time,
they made a pact with the wind.
And from the kitchen table,
I can see the shadows shift
as the pecan breathes in the sunlight.
I wonder if this giant,
the grandfather of our back field,
still has what it takes
under those tendons of bark,
the layers riddled by seasons of birds,
or if the young dogwood tipped with green
will surprise us next March.

There's a deaf kid down the street
who can imitate the passion-
sounds of trees, the groan
and creak of branches so well
that he frightens the old Southern ladies.
Like the wind, he runs a clean path
up their driveways, or drops his bike
and watches for hours as I tear
the weeds, the heart-shaped leaves
of creeper from the gray coiled trunks.
Sometimes, he is so quiet and serious
that I stop what I'm doing
and take a second look.

It is true that we hear
what we want. Yet, these tears
are not for the silence between us
or the shriek of limbs suddenly bared
to the day's dazzling light.
They are the loving itch
of bud and dust, germ and sugar,
the little urges of oak and ash.
Like the vines, I accept their invitations.
I let my own green rags fall
to the ground, believing the sky
will meet all our demands.

MEN BACK THEN

The day began with swallows diving
from palm to palm. In the morning breeze,
the fronds shimmied and the smallest flew
before they knew the air.

There were men back then
who thought they could fly.
For a handout, they scaled the rubbery necks
and the children watched as the flat
yellow wings fell slowly to earth.
And the one who lost his grip—
we heard it all, the shriek
of gravity, the birds passing
like white hands into the sky.

When I woke, I told her my dreams
and she told me which ones would come true.
Two strokes of powder caught
the sunlight crossing the room,
wrapping its arms around her.
She tied the corset, pulled
the stockings off a chair,
and followed that shaft of light
downstairs where the blossoms and nightingales
still slept on the Persian rug.

The first Monday of every month,
another man came to the house—
an Armenian who took the rug and beat it

until the birds funneled in indigo
and the violets tossed their meek hearts
to the wind. As he rolled it out
again on the bare wood floor,
his fingers gobbled up their share
of wool, a coarse dark hole
he finally entered, proving
sometimes a man can fly.

I grew to think each day is swallowed that fast
by the night before or after.
And for every man who wakes up poor,
a woman who wakes lonely.
But she showed me how to shell
the hard shiny egg
and hold the glass bowl up to the light.
When the white diffused, I could see
all the sides of day,
those old nests glowing and shadowless.
Just then, her cloth lifted the dust
off the highest keys on the piano
and another knocked at the door—
a man who could tune pianos,
whose tunes could lift your feet,
whose voice drifted up
through those gold and dying branches
and stole our hearts.

OI-DLE-DOI-DLE-DOI

Your first song to the stream of light
you drink with milk each morning.
A mockingbird spins its litter
of feathers and steals the rest.
Suddenly, he appears before you
in your highchair: spectacles,
a woolen shirt too warm for May.
His breath smelling of wine
and varnish, he croons back,
oy, oy, my little one,
like the faithful chorus
over his grave forty years ago.

He stoops to study your face
and I try to explain that
he is your great–great–grandfather
on your father's side,
a carver of bars
who left his wife and children
to make roses in America.
He blows the dust of birch and cherry,
of Russian forests from his nails,
and smooths your cheek, *eat more . . .*
More! As though pleading could fatten
those palms and knees rubbed raw
from chasing wings of dust
across the floor.

It is rare, I think, such tenderness
and nerve in a man—
enough to make a woman follow him

from one land to another.
Eggs, a little herring, tea.
I give him these
and ask what door in this house
I've left open for him,
and how he came to find our street
from that steamy Concourse in the Bronx,
that loop of virgin trees
outside of Czernowitz.

But he answers in another language,
blessing the trees and this child
who sings into his ghostly ears.
We hear the angel close the door
a second time. How quickly,
the sun takes his place,
the mockingbird sings
as she shreds a crown of phlox
and silences her young.

THE MORAVIAN CEMETERY:
"GOD'S ACRE"

I kneel down, rub the veil
of rain like a balm
into the cold black stone
and read the name, *Anne,*
the mother of three sons,
carved out by a man
who never touched her cheek
or lips, or asked
how life goes on.

But it never ends for those
who always knew where
they were going. For *Jacob,*
tobacco merchant,
the slab of fescue rolls out,
a plot in the next world.
I think a pious man
would have looked down
this long row of stones,
into the valley of cedars
and elms, and seen himself
and kept silent.

Yet, these plain marble faces
make me nervous. Scrubbed clean
each spring, they shone
in rain a hundred years
before the Greeks, the Blacks,
and Baptists entered this graveyard

with their scrolls and trumpet flowers.
The truth does not rest.
It paces the ragged path
past the mounds behind me,
waiting for one man
who refused to die,
who simply *fell asleep*
in 1871.

The shudder of sparrows
will not wake him,
nor the wind that lifts
a stash of seeds from the grass
and carries them off.
There are some secrets
the sky keeps to itself.

THE LAST GIFT

I

The husk of the cicada curls
in air that is thin and pure.
Rain carries the scent of mold and bark,
the last seeds into the earth.

Everyone is waiting for the leaves
to change, for their dead ones
to come back and repeat the end
in a way they can live with.
But sumac is the most beautiful,
offering itself only once.
My hands throb from the cold
as I gather it.

When we left the West,
you promised real seasons—
the mingling of sugar and air.
But the surge of blood to the skin
ends quickly, and an early darkness
waits at our door.

Tonight, when you come home
to this old house wreathed in smoke
and fiber, I will be singing to myself
as I sweep the porch, singing
to the long red leaves the wind scatters.
Even now, they keep their color.
And I am learning to love
what is coming as much as I loved
what was before.

II

Today, it is your turn
to leave the house and learn
the task of healing.
I have told you what a woman knows:
the herbs for cold, stones
for tremor, the way a hand
revives the cheek.

As you cross the street
that leads into this dying city,
I wave and laugh as the spirit
of ice laughs from its tower
in the branches. Leaves fly up,
sticking to your cuffs, your flannel shirt,
and heavy boots that tick
with each step—sycamore,
oak, red maple, amber.
Old wounds, they will never mend.

After mine, the lips you touch
will be gray and silent,
a shapeless nest
unable to hold November.
And when you rest your hands
on the sleeping man's belly,
preparing to bare the withered nerve,
you will see the door through which
darkness enters and breath leaves

and enters you,
carrying a lantern that lights your face.

III

The old woman next door
opens her apron and scours the grass
for the last souring pomegranates.
She might say, "winter ain't no love story."
But then, she won't survive it.

Starlings circle around her.
The red seeds slip through her fingers,
threatening the ice.
They spread like laughter
over this brittle universe. I laugh too
when you liken the curve of my belly
to a freckled gourd
someone has left on our doorstep.

And when she asks how long
we plan to stay,
I say through winter, into spring
when the magnolia opens,
like an angel clapping its white hands.

IV

At last, the sky breaks open.
For the first time,
we are living in houses of snow
and wearing the sky.
Who has sent these flakes?
I make my marks quickly. By noon,
they will be buried like dry twigs.

And what of an old woman
the snow makes young again?
She unlaces the hard brown shoes,
rolls down her stockings
and steps lightly through clouds
into a world we haven't yet seen.
Vested in ice, two firs
stand watch at her door.
Nothing shows itself
but a silence that is named
after the missing.

I want them back: the woman,
the words that stand up like grass
under the sun's red stain,
and those hands that can thaw
the slow rivers of my body,
searching for a season
no one has found.

PART TWO

CHARTRES

1

Tuesday, the most human of days,
and the rain and wind
have left a path of broken geraniums
to the church. Inside, two nuns
from a Breton abbey pass in silence.
The hard white wings of their bonnets
brush against each other.
The air figure-eights
across the vaulted ceiling, wedding
stones so dark I can't see their faces.
Yet, I believe how tall that darkness is,
its huge blue eyes teared
by rain and the labor of hands
that laid each pane in place
at such great heights.

2

As a child, I could never pray
in front of others.
But there were shapes in the night
I could run my hand the length of
until I entered those glowing scenes
inside myself. This evening,
in another room, the moon hangs
prisms in the chestnuts.
The sky is sleeping,
wrapped in its pelt of stars,
and you and I in that darkness so tall

it must stoop to offer its love.
Soon, we will leave as we came,
for the arc of our bodies
over quiet space is the first window.

MAP FOR THE UNBORN

1

He pulled me up from the bed of goldenrod
and with a few quick strokes
brushed the grass, the yellow sparks
from my hair and shoulders.
The road entered the mountains
like a twisted key, letting light
into the darkened valley of cedar and oak.
When we asked *how far to Vernazza,*
the old man's fingers arched over the sea.
Another going the opposite way
simply shrugged and slapped the insects
off his thighs. Finally, a family,
mostly mothers and daughters,
gave many directions. The wind was confused
for these hills had many paths
and the sea spun a thousand threads
in one day. A woman could wear
the same dress her whole life
and still bear a dozen
who would vanish everywhere.

2

After nine months,
you will avoid the heat of the road,
the carelessness of strangers
to travel by water.
There is a small boat rocking
in the cove. Soon, you will slip
the dark rope from its mooring

and row as far as anyone can,
through the curve of fin and bone.

They say no one turns back
on this voyage, though a few swallow
too much sky or water,
and others cry out for nights after.
But then, who remembers these things?

Who remembers the blade of stars
pointing the way,
stars that will fall on the blackened tides
and shine even there, like the eyes
of those who are coming to us?

3

We can only dream of the fingers
of land tying the seas together,
and these dreams are our only maps.

Follow the line that runs
from the thumb to the heart
until lines cover your face
and your legs give in.
Circle the mound of your smallest finger
twice around the world
until your fortune comes and goes
and a villager opens his window
to call you inside.

•

He will take your hand
and ask to hear your stories,
for you have crossed the seas
of your mother, and who can remember
having traveled so far?

RUE MADAME

When the light touches ground,
he's out shuffling under the chestnuts,
banging on the broken shutters.
His trousers inhale and flare,
finning the air behind him—
a fish out of water, they say.
The green bristles pool
under his chin and the aroma
of black Basque mussels escapes
when he walks too quickly.
From a family with too many
small fries to keep him.
But Marcel is his friend.
He pushes the water from the abattoir
to the curb with a stiff broom
and says that no man is a fish.
He claims he's more like the old
trotters sent into the city,
for he often rolls his head half-circle
to watch the sky end on a knoll.
And the boys who steal the cigarettes
Marcel gives him call him a frog.
Always, the warts on his nose,
the bubble of phlegm, the flies . . .
Once, I took you out for a stroll
in this city where they'd eat old men
if they had the right sauce.
And on that hard gray ribbon
that ties us together,
he crossed our path and grinned.
He knelt and rubbed his stain

across your eyes, whispering
what a beautiful child, as though
more than the memory had returned.
Before you're old enough to know
what made you laugh that day,
he'll be gone—and with him,
that staff of light,
those gentle creatures
who answer to any name.

THE PRISONERS OF LOCHES

1

One fall, on the journey south
through the central mountains,
Louis studied the nests of falcons
banked, like old helmets,
on the rocky ledges.
He explored deserted lairs
no other man in his party would enter.
Upon returning to Loches in April,
he drew up plans for the smithy
and the word spread quickly in the village
of the iron baskets, trellises
through which men's fingers grew
in the dark, of enormous nests
which hung by chains
from the pitted ceiling of the Martelet.
In these, their king collected
other greatnesses: counts, dukes,
even the Cardinal de la Balue
swung for years, like old songbirds
trapped by their most faithful tunes.

2

Below, the gray waters of the Indre
swelled and the furrows vanished.
The farmers pulled their rakes
through the softened skulls of beet
and onion that brought nothing
in the market. And where
their wives spat, the dust sizzled

for that was what their lord
had given their children to eat.

But the little ones,
dressed like the earth,
gathered leaves into walls.
They plucked the hen's rump
and crossed the feathers into signs—
all bishops and cardinals
at any age. The trick
was to whistle in high notes
that would rise 500 feet,
like invisible birds, crossing
the watchpath of the Martelet.

And if a sudden breeze carried their trills
as far as the children hoped,
it carried Balue to madness
for he knew that God never lied
and certainly this meant
He was coming to save him.

3

I want to know if it is snowing.
For eleven seasons of snow
will pass, and I have already lost
its color, that trace of whiteness
that flees from the eye,
exposing the pit where they keep us.

•

My fellow prisoners, Autun and Le Puy,
have confirmed my fears. They say
another perished when they led him
from the darkness of his cage
into the sunlight, and offered freedom.
They say his mind caved in.
They are preparing for it,
chinking a small altar
into the damp red stone where
they will leave their prayers
when their own hearts are pierced
by the sudden blade,
or what others call
the day.

4

Now, Louis is dead and the Indre runs
a different course, snaking away
from the sodden walls, the shadows
of robes and chains, into the valley,
the tender channels of plum and grape.
Only an old man is left
to lock the tower and train the roses
skyward with his swollen thumbs.
I am the last to leave the dungeon.
I trace the stain of ash
with my toe, the tattoo
of a torture fire burned forever
into the earth. Years ago,
the French tore down the nests

and fed them to fires
which are heat and ash, then nothing,
no matter where you build them.

And though the sweat has dried
and the wounds, like small red wings,
have flown inward, a scar
of darkness crosses the face
of the man with the keys.
Before he leads me out, he points
to words etched on the wall above me:
celui qui n'est pas contan,
he who is not content.
As I read a second time,
a gust of air which is ancient
passes over and I can almost hear them
spoken in the whisper of rain,
in the rustle of wheat being cut
in the fields. Yes, I answer,
it will soon be snowing.
And I seldom lie.

CINQUE TERRE: THE LAND OF FIVE NOISES

for Shula

In the summer, the Monterossans are even noisier:
the Communists and Socialists, sponge dealers
and women returning home at dark.
Children shout the fish from the shallows,
the rats back into the rocky shadows of the sea wall.
Only lovers get by in silence.

Even in that moment between words
when breath goes up in light
and utterance is impossible,
a motorbike stutters through the village
and two more after it,
or a train thrashes through a mossy gorge
toward the sea. Dreams are unnecessary—
talked away, like the bruised seawater
pulling out of the enormous caves.
Only sleeping stops the rumors
when a trace of color,
like the stain of peppers on muslin,
rushes the motionless faces.

Yet, a few things can be explained
by all this racket. Life must be named,
called back often before it wanders too far.
And so, a mother lifts her skirt
and slowly wades into the water
after a child who would rather follow
the fish to their smoky depths.

•

Also, there are always those
who mean nothing when they speak,
who, like birds, love the sound of air so much
they wave their arms, their tongues
and give it away.

ABOVE THE ARNO

When the sheets are wrung,
the socks and aprons hung moon-wise
above the Arno, her young man
sneaks across to the other side.
In the dark, I cup your chin
and snip the wet black curls off your nape
like a censor blotting out
the commas in a woman's letter.
I let them fall three floors down
to the river or the cobblestones,
to the wings of insects
who dress the statues while we sleep.

For *Cosimo il Vecchio*,
it has been a long ride through his city.
He yawns and stabs his sword
into a melon rind left by a vendor.
At dawn, the blush of sugar
is still on his lips. *David*
hurries down the marble corridor,
past a sleeping guard,
and up the stairs to Nina's place
but Nina's with another.
And *the fat man of the Boboli* digs
his spurs into the flanks of his tortoise,
making haste to the all-night café
where the anarchists meet.
The night is sudden and sure
of itself. As we sleep,
our shadows lighten and we become
more perfect.
•

They say you shouldn't laugh
at history, though a few loose strands
have dried in stubborn smiles
on the back of your head.
Or at its sullen relics,
though I know that out there
on the steets at this very moment
is a woman so poor she talks to the statues
all through the night, and gathers
the butts flicked off the balconies,
the bits of hair for her winter coat.

Those who can't sleep tonight
are watching the moon
between two poplars streaked with carbon.
It refuses to move. Its cold light
comes down and bears witness.

THE SPIRIT OF PAVIA

If you can't fly away
on one of those silver birds
Alitalia sends to the U.S.
or Moscow, can't even rise
in spirit from the crumbling shadows
of a dance hall late Friday night,
rise to the scent of lilac
and petrol on the avenue,
then you must surrender
your clouded eyes,
your spine twisted like the trunk
of the lilac, to this world
where a stool sits by the window,
and sip what the old call
the emerald of Pavia.

Or if you're young, poor,
and too shy to leave the dance hall
with a boy, to weave a sprig
of jasmine into your hair
and ride with him into the faithful
starlight of the countryside;
and if, to make it worse,
you have too many sisters
who know how to find men
without the use of flowers,
then your father sends you to live
with more sisters who have nothing,
nothing but their knowledge of the spirit,
the spirit of Pavia,

that secret blend of flowers
liquefied.

It is the same for the old man
and the novice: the mystery
of an eventual marriage to something
in the clouds, the vow of silence
that curls the tongue.
She kneels under the marble arches of Certosa
and the spilled mop water creeps
up her hem. He slumps
on the warped pew. And they pray
once for their Mother, a second time
for their city, and a third
to be shown the way out of it.

Then, one Friday in an evening Mass,
while the rest are out dancing,
the cherubs painted on the ceiling
drift down over the two bowed heads.
They have been sickened by incense,
by the sweet smile of the great Visconti
sleeping in stone, and the centuries
of watching his enemies boiled
until their bones were as shiny
and cold as the cross. They cry
Get out! . . . *Leave now while you're young,*
for even in the eyes of children
they are both still young.

•

And they follow the cherubs
out of the church, into the summer night
leading north, away from their country.
The girl sees the starlight
grazing a wheat field.
The old man hears the poplars
whispering over the road.
And the few who have joined them
tell of a lake they will pass
with water as pure and green
as that emerald. The night goes on
like this until the old man begins
to shiver and sing to himself,
until the novice, tucking her skirts
around her ankles, traces each star
like a bead on her chain.

And the cherubs huddle in a pink cloud
above them, laughing
as one opens a flask
and they take turns putting it
to their lips—this memory,
this dream—laughing
at how far it has gotten them.

THE OLD CITY

After the sun goes down,
you can hear the insects in the walls
of this old hotel—300-year-old ants,
roaches still wearing the royal colors,
demanding the dust be swept from their villas,
issuing orders someone must carry out.

Downstairs,
the young dishwasher steps out of the steam,
the streak of silver and china,
to take a break in the alley.
He shares his cigarette with the night.
The women sitting by their windows
peer into the darkness,
their arms folded on the sills
like soft ocher stones.

They study the night
to see how far they have to go
before their work is done.

The street winds forever
through rooms that are coming from dust
and going back to it.
The shadows are huge and endless
as the song of a young man
whose voice can't crack the walls,
send anyone into hiding,
or bring silence,
for this world is never finished.

THE BRIDGE OF
SAINT-BÉNÉZET

Sur le pont d'Avignon
on y danse, on y danse . . .

I pinch the flame
and the milky stump drowns slowly
into itself. Often,
the night joins us before the streets
of Avignon are quiet
and the day's newspaper has blown
into the river, blurring
under the wash of stars.

Above the Rhône,
the popes sold their blessings
and the sun went down every night
for a hundred and thirty years
as though light were gold
and the frail reeds could bear
its weight. The bastard children
left their mothers' houses
and climbed the path in darkness
to the palace where he waited.
For each, a sermon,
the nudge of a grizzled cheek
turned on a satin pillow.
But, at dawn, only Bénézet,
the little one with no real father
or mother, saw the angel of stone
crossing the river and heard it
calling his name.

The bridge where the children danced
has crumbled into the water,

the wreath of voices whisked downstream.
The new day's sun presses the night
back into its wicks, the charred trunks
wading in slowly. And the children
who once edged their way past the hawkers
and carts laden with onions
are now this green finger
that touches the sea.

I think they must have hidden
down those endless cobbled streets,
their shoes and baskets emptied
of light as each wooden door
slammed shut for the last time.
Or wandered off into the groves
east of here after pears or small birds
that let themselves be caught.
And yet, on nights when the wind
flushes the swallows down in the grass,
the current changes.
You can see the delicate craw of a branch
almost wave as it floats by,
or a face from long ago
rise in an eddy. The silt swirls
over your boots as you kneel,
leaning to pull them out.

And, like the stars, out they come.

FISHES AT SAINT-JEAN: CHAGALL, 1949

I

Because the sea is also
in me, a sea so blue
that parrots fly through it
and horses and other women
who are true, I want to dive
and feel the ragged edges
of your canvas folding over me
like water.

On the ocean floor
the grass is swaying,
the horses are diminished
and delicate, and a mollusk
drifts between two lovers
fighting the urge
to rise. But up here,
the light freezes the ivory walls
of the museum. The guard sleeps
with his hands in his pockets.
And the woman selling tickets
drowns in her cubicle,
the hard bubbles rising
from her lips toward the sun.
No one saw it sneaking in
through a diamond of glass,
etching its path of light.
As I follow, the seas part
and all the beautiful blind fish
are thrown at my feet.

•

If color
is the secret you share,
there are other things
I could tell you,
things that would please you
more than sapphires
or crushed tourmalines,
more than the indigo veins
of fish or birds, the infinite
drops of seawater, more
than the final blue note
of an accordion that carries us
through the warm night air.

II

Like an acrobat in a green suit,
the wave lifts, spins, and lets go.
And then another follows.

The small stones clap softly
at the water's edge
where I press a mold for my body
and lie back, letting
the day's heat enter. They say
the agate of flesh inside me
will one day spin out,
floating beyond the children
catching foam in their arms,
beyond the last lacy swell

to a place where the water
barely moves and you are sculling
belly-up, like a great whale
filled with rooms of air
and darkness.

At the day's end, the sun
lifts its nets off the water
and the moon rises. You swim in
and find me still staring out—
the lights on the barges and the new stars
becoming the same. Perhaps
I will find my way back here tonight
while you are sleeping,
like other women who have left their homes
for these slashed shores. And like another,
I'll make a wreath of stones
for a small fire which, like the sea,
is the mother of all colors.

Though memories dissolve
in the waves of darkness, many nights
have been passed this way—
a woman waiting it out
who can only guess how much of herself
she has given to this world.

III

It's true.
My belly will soon be as round

as the dazed summer moon
or the lush little islands
off the coast.

You smile and tip
the scored carafe of cassis
into both our glasses.
Now the crowds are filling
the cafés along the promenade,
angels wrapped in gauze
against the gentlest breeze.
Even flies dance on the light bulbs
and old women peek at themselves
in the gritty mirrors behind the bar.

You don't want others
looking at me the way they do—
men with eyes as quick as fish
or those saying nothing
as they melt into their own reflections
on the table next to us.
I like cassis,
the currant-red of the hills
along the sea where I dreamed
mermaids live in winter, knitting
by fires as red as this glass.

I can't hold it in any longer.
It is as round as the storm cloud
that sailed over as you swam
into shore. The patron

unrolls the awning to the curb
and a light rain collects
the softened faces at the edge
of our vision. We look for one
with a message, the face
of a gypsy child who has your eyes
and plays a painted fiddle.

In his dish, coins
stamped with the names
of the old world we're in,
and one with the name
of the new world in me.

NOTES

"The Prisoners of Loches": A fortress and prison located in the Loire Valley of France, inhabited by the counts of Anjou. It was known for its cages, which were built by Louis XI to confine his prisoners. The Cardinal de la Balue, a counselor to Louis XI, was held prisoner in one of the cages for eleven years after he was caught betraying the king.

"The Spirit of Pavia": Certosa di Pavia, located in Pavia, Italy, is a Carthusian Monastery that was founded in 1396 by Gian Galeazzo Visconti of Milan.

"The Bridge of Saint-Bénézet": Located in Avignon, France, the seat of the papacy from 1309 to 1377, this bridge was popularized by the nursery rhyme. Legend has it that in 1177, a young shepherd boy, Bénézet, was commanded by voices from heaven to build a bridge across the river at a spot indicated by an angel. He proved to others that he was inspired by miraculously lifting a huge block of stone.